Emotional Resilience
Learning to Process Emotions

Copyright © 2021 by Erienne Luck. All rights reserved.

ISBN: 9798720201012

Distribution and reproduction are strictly prohibited by law.
It's also bad karma.

First Edition. No part of this publication may be reproduced,
stored in a retrieval system, or transmitted in any form,
or by any means, electronic, mechanical, photocopying,
recorded, scanning or otherwise,
without permission of the author or publisher.

Requests to the author should be addressed to
Erienne Luck

For information about reprint rights, translation,
bulk purchases, or to find
other books please contact **info.luckesoul@gmail.com**

Once there was a little angel named Tian
who was confused and upset by the weather.

Sometimes the clouds would cry and cry and cry
as water poured down their cheeks in waves
to the earth below, so she would cover her eyes too, and
block out the water.

Sometimes, the clouds would be gone altogether and it was just miles and miles of baby blue sky, so Tian was all smiles and grinned from ear to ear.

Other times the wind would howl and screech at the sky all night long and so she would lay awake in her bed, staring at the back of her eyelids, unable to sleep.

Sometimes the thunder would boom and
shout so loudly, that she would cover her ears and hide.
The powerful sound scared her.

The wind would chase the clouds across the sky all night,
and she would feel as though she could
not breathe well enough.

Sometimes the wind would just whisper silly things in her ears and tickle her toes.

Tian would laugh and laugh until she felt like she could not breathe well enough.

Her favorite was when the sunshine and the rain took turns singing songs to each other. They created a beautiful harmony which filled her belly with warm waves of energy.

Tian didn't understand the weather, but that didn't stop the weather from coming to play with her.

One day, as she lay in her bed, she heard the thunder begin shouting loudly at the sky. She plugged her ears and covered her head with a fluffy blanket. She couldn't hear a thing, and that made her feel a little better.

She decided to stop listening to weather because it was unpredictable and so unpleasant. She stuffed lots of fluff in her ears and ignored the moody weather.

After some time, she stopped noticing the weather.
She didn't hear the thunder shouting. She stopped noticing the rain against her cheeks. She even ignored the tightness in her empty chest when she was not breathing well.

She stopped noticing the sunshine.
She didn't remember to notice the wind as it desperately tried to get her attention or the rain that begged for a smile. Tian began to feel heavy and sad. She didn't know why she felt heavy and sad, but she did. She felt very HEAVY, and she felt very SAD, and she did not know why.

She wanted to tell others how sad and heavy life felt, but most of them had fluff in their ears too or their eyes were looking down, so they weren't able to see her. The others were busy, busy, busy!

They didn't have time to listen to her, or pay her any attention, and so she stopped asking for help. She sat down and wondered what to do. No one seemed to care about her feelings, and she didn't know what was causing her heavy sadness. She thought for a while and decided that it was time to take a little vacation from the life she was living.

She decided to visit the desert. When she arrived, she noticed how hot the desert was. "Great!" she thought grumpily, "Perhaps this wasn't what I needed after all".

She sat down with a heavy thud in the sand, pulled the fluff from her ears and tossed it away. It took a few minutes for her eyes and ears to adjust to her surroundings. She sat still and quietly looked around just observing.

Then slowly she heard the quiet humming of tiny wings. The sound came from a small delicate blue and green hummingbird as he whizzed through the bright clear air. He was floating from flower to flower on a tall green poky cactus covered in giant yellow blossoms, drinking the sweet juice inside the flower.

She noticed a lanky black stink bug that lumbered over the soft sand with his bum high in the air. She put her hands into the soft sand herself and felt the tiny warm beads of sand slipping through her fingers like silk. She smelled the savory scent of a dusty sagebrush as she reached underneath it, in search of the cricket who was singing softly.

She felt a bit of happiness begin flowing inside her belly, as she carefully peeled a bright red prickly pear fruit and ate it. She felt her joy growing again when the soft tender flesh of the prickly pear squished against her lips making the juice run down her cheek. Tian stayed all afternoon in the desert just exploring, touching, smelling and observing the things in nature.

She was so absorbed in her new experience that she didn't notice the huge black clouds that the wind began to drag across the blue desert sky. She hardly noticed the small cool droplets of rain and their pitter patter on the sand at first, but as it does in the desert, small drops turned into enormous drops, and in a downpour, water began to cover everything.

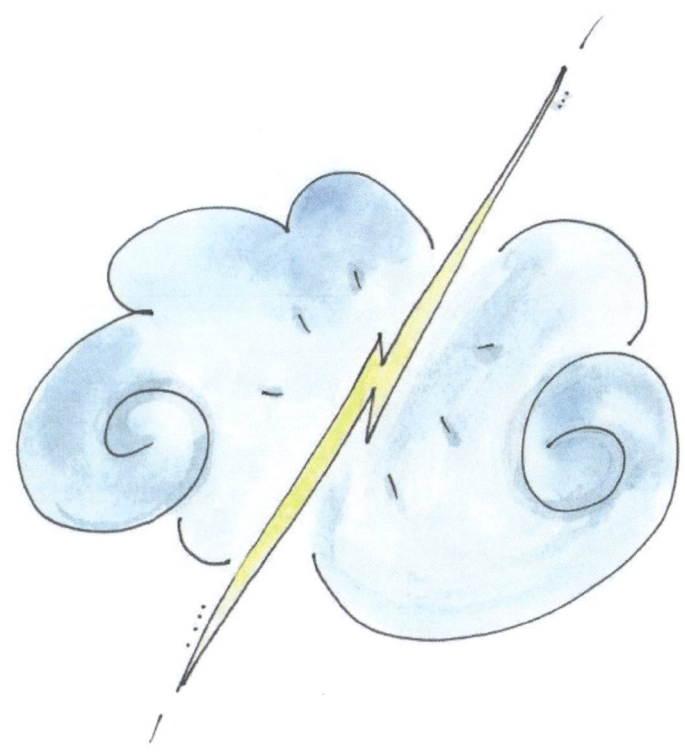

She felt the sting on her cheeks as wind hurled sand through the air and dashed against her skin. She stopped short of breath, her heart pounding in her chest, as she looked up to see lightening flash across the sky. Then came thunder. The moments before it boomed, she felt an eternity pass slowly away, and there it was.

The thunder began to shout at the sky and all of the horrible feelings came back in a rushed wave of cold heat that started at her toes and washed up to her wet burning cheeks. Thunder! Terrible awful thunder. Thunder so loud that she felt she had nowhere to go and nowhere to hide.

Tian stood in the desert wet, sad, afraid, and dripping with fear. Then, as it often does in the desert, the storm began to calm itself. The wind began to drag the dark clouds somewhere else. The tempest had lasted only a short time. It was gone as quickly as it came.

Tian began to look around her. The hummingbird fluffed his feathers dry. The stink bug crawled down from the glistening wet rocks, and the dusty desert sagebrush smelled of happiness once more as the cricket began to chirp his tiny song.

Tian began to finally understand, and so will you,
that life is not about blocking out the weather, but learning
to enjoy all the experiences it brings.

Tian decided she wouldn't cover her eyes when the
water came. She decided she wouldn't put fluff in
her ears any longer. She decided she would dance in the
rain. She would feel the wind. She would listen to the thunder.
She would smile to the sunshine even when it was
hiding behind the clouds.

Tian left the desert and went back home.
When she arrived, the fluffy white clouds tickled
her feet and teased her for leaving home.

What is Emotional Resilience?

Emotional resilience is becoming aware of your emotions and allowing the resulting physical sensations to flow freely through and out of your body, without it resulting in huge or uncontrollable reactions. Recognizing emotions as opportunities for personal growth can allow you to easily navigate your life experience, which is guaranteed to be filled with all kinds of emotions.

Emotions can keep you safe from harm. Emotions, like love, create soul connections so you feel close to others. Emotions are the key to creating friendships with people. Emotions can help you set limits for yourself, so you can explore ways to avoid potential problems. Emotions are nature's guidance system that let you know when to keep doing what you are doing and when to stop and change what you are doing.

Listen to your feelings with a wish to understand and support your own existence. Practice finding names for emotional feelings and locating places they cause physical tension during each emotion you feel. Emotions flow better when you are able to use words to describe the experience you are having. When you listen to your own feelings, you can safely deal with them inside or effectively share them with others if you wish.

Learn Emotional Resilience

1. **OBSERVE**
NOTICE your thoughts. Notice the physical sensations in your body. Notice your own actions. Thoughts, emotions, and impulses to take action come through little messengers in your body called hormones. These are chemicals made by special cells that get released into your bloodstream. Your brainwaves tell your body when to release theses chemicals so your body knows what to do and when.

2. **DESCRIBE**
Locate **WHERE** you feel tension or physical sensation in your body. Speak it out loud or tell your parents **WHAT** you are experiencing. Give your body a quick little squeeze or gentle pat on that area. Release built up emotion or trauma stored in your system and stop more from getting stuck, by taking a deep breaths and relaxing your whole body. Your emotions are designed to flow through you but not stick to you. Just let them happen without taking action while you notice, then describe them. Practice using 3-4 words to describe each emotion's sensation you experience from the lists found on pages 21-22.

3. **APPRECIATE**
Emotions are the unspoken language of your spirit and body working together. They are simply giving you information or guidance. Guidance that lets you know if you should stop and change what you are doing or if you should keep doing what you're doing. Remember, always **THANK** your body for sharing such precious information, and.....
never try to hurt your body when it shares emotions with you.

Emotional Resilience

The Key to Unlocking Your Internal Universe

For CHILDREN to Memorize

That's a program, it's not me.
I feel it (**WHERE**). It feels like (**WHAT**).
Thank you, (**NAME**), for allowing me to experience this.
I love you, and I completely accept you!

For PARENTS to Memorize

That is a thought program, it's not actually you.
You are just observing the temporary emotional feeling called _"fear"_.
What is your body physically feeling right now?
_"heart beating fast in my chest, shaking and sweaty hands,
wave of heat on my cheeks"_ because of _"fear"_.
Thank you _"child's name"_ for sharing your feelings with me.
I love you, and I complete accept you!

*Children fill in the blanks, adults speak the rest*

HEAVY FEELINGS

Emotion

aggressive
angry
afraid
alarmed
annoyed
bitter
bored
disgusted
dominated
discouraged
dissatisfied
distressed
doubtful
embarrassed
empty
fearful
frustrated
frazzled
guilty
hopeless
hesitant

insulted
irritated
lonely
miserable
negative
offended
paralyzed
pathetic
powerless
sad
shameful
shy
stressed
resentful
rage
tense
tired
uncertain
upset
useless
vulnerable

Sensation

burning
cold
dark
electric
hard
heavy
hot
intense
itchy
large
loud
painful
pressure
rough
sharp
shaky

sweaty
small
soft
sore
sticky
stiff
stuck
tense
twitching
tight
tingling
pins & needles
undulating
unpleasant
vibrating
waves

_____   _____
_____   _____
_____   _____

Add your own to the list

LIGHT FEELINGS

Emotion

accepting
affectionate
alive
amazed
attracted
bold
brave
calm
courageous
comfortable
confident
content
daring
delighted
devoted
energetic
excited
enthusiastic
fascinated
festive
fortunate
free

grateful
glad
happy
hopeful
important
joyful
motivated
open
playful
peaceful
powerful
productive
quiet
relaxed
serene
surprised
sympathetic
thrilled
understanding
wise
willing

Sensation

cool
expanding
firm
flowing
floating
free
growing
intense
large
light
open
peaceful
quiet

satisfying
small
smooth
soft
soothing
strong
tingling
vibrating
warm
waves
wild

_____ _____
_____ _____
_____ _____

Add your own to the list

A Lifetime of Practice

Practice emotional resilience daily. As you practice letting feelings flow through you, you are on your way to allowing your system to operate as nature designed it to. Remember, you allow your feelings to freely flow through and out of your body by deeply relaxing. Start to relax your body by closing your eyes and taking several long deep breaths.

Let's practice. Close your eyes.

Take in a few deep breaths......(pause to let child practice)

Good! Notice your body feeing more relaxed?

You can unlearn any conditioned emotional response by deeply relaxing your body, breathing in and out, and holding still until the feeling has passed all the way through your body. Musical sounds help this process along. You really can heal emotional hurt. Real healing includes not "picking at a healing scab" so make sure to practice making things right.

You are in control of your thoughts + actions

Allow your emotions to flow through you, not stick to you

Making Things Right While Learning

Learning emotional resilience is usually challenging at first. So what do you do when you make a mistake while you are learning? Make things right! Ho'oponopono is a Hawaiian forgiveness technique meaning to make things right. You will want to practice making things right while learning to be good at regulating your emotions, because it helps create emotional intelligence.

I learned Ho'oponopono when I was just a little girl, although we used another word. The word I learned is *repentance*. Both forgiveness techniques help you make things right after you make a mistake. You can learn to make things right. Practicing will help you to stay positive, happy, and present in the moment, and this usually makes things right.

4 Phrases For Making Things Right

I am sorry: This is what you say to let someone know you are aware what you did was hurtful.

Please forgive me: This is how you ask someone if they would be willing to stop feeling angry or resentful toward you when you make mistake. Always let them know you also plan on stopping and correcting your actions.

Thank you: This is a way to let others know you are gratefully accepting what is being offered.

I love you: This is what you say to let others know you are devoted to being kind to them no matter how many mistakes are made.

Put On Emotional Armor With Happy Thoughts

Happy thoughts put on your emotional armor. Each emotional feeling you have is temporary. Emotions are like hills and valleys. Some take you up to new heights while others take you down into new depths. Emotions are beneficial and have the ability to create a wonderful, positive, foundation for a better life experience, but only if you allow them to freely flow through your body. This can be a really unpleasant experience. Sometimes emotions feel just plain awful, especially the heavy, dark, and sticky kind. It really helps if you stop and truly notice them, describe where they happen, then appreciate your experience.

Remember, you can allow your feelings to flow all the way through and out of your body by deeply relaxing. You can even give the area of sensation in your body a little pat or squeeze with your hand to let your body know you hear it. Maybe you will try it and start to feel happier than you have ever been before, or maybe you won't try it all. This choice is all yours.

Smile, relax, and begin to feel good about this experience called being you. Don't take the words or actions of others as a personal attack, become upset, or repeat them in your mind. If you do they create emotional scars.

Happy thoughts help you put on emotional armor and create mental harmony. Remember, thoughts and feelings go together. Experiencing all kinds of temporary emotional feelings are essential to a fulfilling life. Emotions are the soil that thoughts and ideas grow in. This is why it is important to have healthy soil. Happy thoughts can heal emotionally traumatic scars and prevent new ones. Simply practice deeply relaxing when you feel upset to activate your body's natural super powers.

Practice Increasing Your Happy

1. Practice having a positive mental attitude. (PMA)

2. Practice feeling and acting friendly towards others, especially if you don't feel like it.

3. Practice being less critical and more tolerant of others, their faults, failings, and mistakes. We all have something to get better at.

4. Have the best possible interpretation for the actions of others.

5. Think and behave as though what you want is going to happen.

6. Practice acting like you are already the sort of person you wish to become.

7. Create a new habit to replace an old yucky habit.

8. Practice not taking things as a personal attack.

9. Practice EMOTIONAL RESILINACE everyday.

10. Practice smiling every day, multiple times a day.

11. Practice reacting to the actions of others calmly.

12. Practice refusing to think pessimistic or negative things about people or events you can do nothing to change. You have better things to think about.

13. Practice being consciously committed to happiness every day.

14. Acknowledge that you are not perfect or proficient upon first attempt and you will keep practicing until it is quite easy to feel happy, regardless of what happens around you.

15. Never give up hope. Tomorrow is new and so are you!

What My Emotions Feel Like

Emotion Name	Emotion Feel Like	Where Feel
_____	_____+_____+_____	_____
_____	_____+_____+_____	_____
_____	_____+_____+_____	_____
_____	_____+_____+_____	_____
_____	_____+_____+_____	_____
_____	_____+_____+_____	_____
_____	_____+_____+_____	_____
_____	_____+_____+_____	_____
_____	_____+_____+_____	_____
_____	_____+_____+_____	_____
_____	_____+_____+_____	_____
_____	_____+_____+_____	_____
_____	_____+_____+_____	_____
_____	_____+_____+_____	_____
_____	_____+_____+_____	_____

About the Author

Erienne Luck was born in St. George, Utah, in May of 1983. She was raised by loving and supportive parents Brad and Lori Beatty in Hurricane, Utah, near Zion National Park.

Her linguistic and artistic skills began to develop early in life. She learned to speak with great clarity at an early age and began to excel in the arts at an early age also. Her mother noticed this talent around age 5, and put her in local after school art programs, which encouraged the further development of these talents.

She was enrolled in college art classes by age 15 and was able to learn from masterful teachers such as Del Parson and Glen Blakley. She later graduated with an Associate of Art from Dixie State University at age 20.

Her books were planted as a seed in her early life, as a suggestion from her mother. Her mother felt that an individual who could both write and illustrate their own books would be quite favorable. Almost two decades later, Erienne finally decided to water that little seed and grow some beautiful books.

Erienne is fascinated with little people. She is inspired by their tenacity and vibrancy. She encourages everyone to emulate the abilities of children, as they attract that which they truly desired into their life without words. They communicate without adulteration, the beautiful messages, that come from the sincere of heart.

She has two beautiful children of her own, a son and a daughter, for which her stories were born and told many times before they reached your eyes and ears. You too, can enjoy her stories like her own children do. As she often refers to herself as the mother of happiness, you can become a child of happiness, as you learn to grow beautiful dreams to pass on for your own legacy.

Printed in Great Britain
by Amazon